The Teaching Assistant's Pocket Guide to Differentiation

By Mike Gershon

D1369115

About the Author

Mike Gershon is known in the United Kingdom and beyond as an expert educationalist whose knowledge of teaching and learning is rooted in classroom practice. His online teaching tools have been viewed and downloaded more than 3.5 million times, making them some of the most popular of all time.

He is the author of over 100 books and guides covering different areas of teaching and learning. Some of Mike's bestsellers include books on assessment for learning, questioning, differentiation, growth mindsets and stretch and challenge. You can train with Mike online, from anywhere in the world, via TES Institute. He regularly delivers CPD and INSET in schools across the UK and Europe.

Find out more at www.mikegershon.com

Training and Consultancy

Mike offers a range of training and consultancy service covering all areas of teaching and learning, raising achievement and classroom practice. Examples of recent training events include:

- Using Growth Mindsets to Develop Resilient Learners

- AfL Unlocked: Practical Strategies for Classroom Success

- Stretching and Challenging More-Able Learners

- Effective Questioning: Developing a Toolkit of Strategies to Raise Achievement

- Differentiating for Whole-Class Teaching

To find out more, visit:

www.mikegershon.com

www.gershongrowthmindsets.com

Or get in touch via mike@mikegershon.com

Other Works from the Same Author

Available to buy now on Amazon:

The Teaching Assistant's Pocket Guide Series:

The Teaching Assistant's Pocket Guide to Growth Mindsets

The Teaching Assistant's Pocket Guide to Questioning

The Teaching Assistant's Pocket Guide to Feedback

The Teaching Assistant's Pocket Guide to Differentiation

The Teaching Assistant's Pocket Guide to Assessment for Learning

The Teaching Assistant's Pocket Guide to Supporting Less-Able Learners

The Teaching Assistant's Pocket Guide to Positive Behaviour Management

The Teaching Assistant's Pocket Guide to Metacognition

The Teaching Assistant's Pocket Guide to Supporting EAL Learners

The Teaching Assistant's Pocket Guide to Teaching and Learning

The 'How To...' Series:

How to use Differentiation in the Classroom: The Complete Guide

How to use Assessment for Learning in the Classroom: The Complete Guide

How to use Bloom's Taxonomy in the Classroom: The Complete Guide

How to use Questioning in the Classroom: The Complete Guide

How to Develop Growth Mindsets in the Classroom: The Complete Guide

How to use Discussion in the Classroom: The Complete Guide

How to Manage Behaviour in the Classroom: The Complete Guide

How to Teach EAL Students in the Classroom: The Complete Guide

How to use Feedback in the Classroom: The Complete Guide

How to be an Outstanding Trainee Teacher: The Complete Guide

The 'Quick 50' Series:

50 Quick Ways to Stretch and Challenge More-Able Students

50 Quick Ways to Create Independent Learners

50 Quick Ways to go from Good to Outstanding

50 Quick Ways to Support Less-Able Learners

50 Quick Ways to Get Past 'I Don't Know'

50 Quick Ways to Start Your Lesson with a Bang!

50 Quick Ways to Improve Literacy Across the Curriculum

50 Quick Ways to Improve Feedback and Marking

50 Quick and Brilliant Teaching Ideas

50 Quick and Brilliant Teaching Techniques

50 Quick and Easy Lesson Activities

50 Quick and Ways to Help Your Students Secure A and B Grades at GCSE

50 Quick and Ways to Help Your Students Think, Learn and Use Their Brains Brilliantly

50 Quick Ways to Motivate and Engage Your Students

50 Quick Ways to Outstanding Teaching

50 Quick Ways to Perfect Behaviour Management

50 Quick and Brilliant Teaching Games

50 Quick and Easy Ways Leaders Can Prepare for Ofsted

50 Quick and Easy Ways to Outstanding Group Work

50 Quick and Easy Ways to Prepare for Ofsted

50 Quick and Easy Ways to Outstanding English Teaching (with Lizi Summers)

50 Quick and Brilliant Ideas for English Teaching (with Lizi Summers)

50 Quick and Easy Ways to Build Resilience through English Teaching (with Lizi Summers)

Other Books:

More Secondary Starters and Plenaries

Secondary Starters and Plenaries: History

How to be Outstanding in the Classroom

Teach Now! History: Becoming a Great History Teacher

The Exams, Tests and Revision Pocketbook

The Growth Mindset Pocketbook (with Professor Barry Hymer)

Series Introduction

The 'Teaching Assistant's Pocket Guide' series developed out of my desire to give teaching assistants across the country a set of practical, useful books they could call on to help them in their work. Having worked with teaching assistants throughout my teaching career and knowing full well the hugely positive impact they can have on learners in a whole variety of different classrooms, I thought it was high time there was a series of books dedicated to supporting them in their working lives.

Each volume in the series focuses on a different aspect of teaching and learning. Each one aims to give teaching assistants a quick, easy way into the topic, along with a wide range of practical strategies and techniques they can use to support, guide and develop the learners with whom they work.

All of the books are designed to help teaching assistants. Each one goes out of its way to make their lives easier, and to help them develop professionally. But, crucially, the ultimate aim of each book is to give teaching assistants the tools they need to better support the learners they spend their time working with.

The whole series is written with the classroom in mind. This is a collection practical of books for what is a practical job.

I hope you find the series useful, interesting and informative. I hope it helps you to develop your work in the classroom and, of course, I hope it helps you to work ever more effectively with your learners on a daily basis.

Acknowledgements

My thanks to all the staff and students I have worked with past and present, including all the teachers and teaching assistants, particularly those at Pimlico Academy and King Edward VI School, Bury St Edmunds. Thanks also to the teachers and teaching assistants who have attended my training sessions and who always offer great insights into what works in the classroom. Finally, thanks to Kall Kwik BSE for their great design work and thanks also to the Education Endowment Foundation for their illuminating research on the role of teaching assistants.

Table of Contents

Chapter 1 – What is differentiation?

Differentiation is all the ways in which teachers or teaching assistants help learners to access the learning, regardless of their starting points. It is about personalising learning, but not to the extent that we have to create lots of different worksheets every lesson. And it is not about planning three different lessons to deliver at the same time, in an effort to ensure every learner in the class can access the work.

Instead, differentiation is about all the strategies and techniques teachers and teaching assistants use to ensure the learners they are working with can make good progress, no matter what the lesson topic. This means differentiation covers all three areas of teaching – planning, teaching and assessment. In each area there are opportunities for personalisation. Opportunities to employ strategies and techniques which help learners to access the work – and to experience a level of challenge that matches where they are currently at.

Let us now put the role of the teacher to one side, however, and focus exclusively on what differentiation means for teaching assistants.

For most teaching assistants, differentiation is focussed on what happens during lessons. This is the time when they are working with learners – whether one-to-one, with small groups, or circulating through the class as a whole.

Differentiation for teaching assistants means finding strategies and techniques through which you can help learners access the learning and make good progress during the lesson. It is about the interactions you have with your learners. These interactions form the basis of the teaching assistant's work. It is through interactions that you help learners, support them and work with them.

During the course of a lesson, teaching assistants have many opportunities for differentiation. That is, they have many opportunities to personalise the learning. To help learners access the learning and make good progress, no matter where they are currently at.

For example, we might have a teaching assistant who is working one-to-one with a learner. This learner finds learning difficult. They are frequently behind their peers and need quite a large amount of extra support. The teaching assistant provides some of this through their interactions with the learner. They help them to access the learning and to make sense of what is going on.

They ask questions, explain ideas, prompt the learner, scaffold the learning, model how to do certain things, and help the learner to verbalise their ideas before writing them down. All of these strategies are examples of differentiation, because they all involve the teaching assistant doing something in an effort to help their learner get to grips with the lesson content. This is what personalisation means.

Another example might see a teaching assistant working with a small group of learners who feel fairly confident with the work they have been set. In this situation, the teaching assistant's role is slightly different. Having checked to see that the learners are not having any difficulties in accessing the work, the teaching assistant takes their role to be about providing an extra level of challenge. They do this by posing questions, suggesting alternative approaches and challenging the learners to develop and expand their work.

These strategies are also part of differentiation, because they involve the teaching assistant finding ways to personalise the learner's experience. This personalisation can involve stretching and challenging learners who find the work easy, as well as supporting learners who find the work difficult.

Before we move on, let's recap:

- Differentiation is all the things we do to help learners access the learning and make good progress, regardless of their starting points.

- Differentiation is therefore all the strategies, activities and techniques we use to make this happen.

- For teaching assistants, differentiation is primarily about the interactions they have with learners during the lesson.

- Differentiation involves helping learners who are struggling to access the work. It also involves stretching and challenging learners who are successfully completing the work.

- Effective differentiation helps personalise learning. This does not mean the lesson or the learning is different for everybody. Instead, it means the teaching assistant is doing different things for different learners to help them access the work and experience an appropriate level of challenge.

It is fair to say, then, that differentiation involves a lot of different things. There are many strategies, activities and techniques we can use to differentiate learning.

In this book, my aim is to present you with a wide range of tools you can call on when you are working with learners, to help you differentiate effectively. Other books in the series will also help you in your efforts. There are natural overlaps between differentiation and questioning, for example, as well as between differentiation and feedback. In both cases, the teaching assistant responds to what learners are doing (through questioning or through feedback) and personalises this as a matter of course.

My aim is to avoid repetition in the pages which follow, so I have left questioning and feedback largely to one side. In addition, the focus in the chapters ahead is more on supporting learners who are struggling to access the learning than on stretching and challenging learners who are finding the work relatively easy. While we do have one chapter on the latter topic, the emphasis is more on the strategies you can use to help learners who need extra support.

To get a better understanding of where we are going, let's take a look at the chapters ahead:

Chapter Two: Essential Techniques for Personalising Learning

Chapter Three: Verbalising Thinking

Chapter Four: Approaches to Explanation

Chapter Five: Scaffolding Strategies

Chapter Six: Modelling Techniques

Chapter Seven: Differentiating Your Questions

Chapter Eight: Increasing the Level of Challenge

Chapter Nine: Memorisation Strategies

Chapter Ten: Conclusion: Recapping and Next Steps

We begin, in Chapter Two, by looking at some of the essentials for personalising learning. These are the techniques you can use in almost any context to help learner's access the learning. They are tools you can call on to help learners get to grips with what is going on.

In Chapter Three, we turn our attention to verbalising thinking. We look at a variety of techniques you can use to help learners articulate, refine and edit their thoughts through speech. Verbalising thinking provides an important way in for many learners. A route through which they can start to make sense of their own thinking.

Chapter Four examines explanation. A range of strategies are presented through which you can explain ideas and information to learners, helping them to understand things which might at first glance have seemed puzzling or confusing. You can use different explanation strategies at different times to help different learners access the lesson content.

In Chapter Five, we look at scaffolding. This is where we do a little bit of the work for our learners, so they can then do the rest of it themselves. These techniques ae all about providing learners with an easier route into the learning. They are akin to taking learners some of the way before saying 'OK, now you go on from here.'

Chapter Six turns the focus to modelling. Modelling is similar to scaffolding but involves a lower level of learner independence. When we model, we show learners what we want them to do or how we want them to think. We provide a model they can imitate, copy or borrow from. This acts as a starting point, helping them to figure out how they can successfully engage with the learning.

In Chapter Seven, we spend a bit of time thinking about how to differentiate questions. This is a brief foray into the topic – giving you just enough to start developing your questioning so it is more personalised and more closely matched to learner needs. For a full review of questioning techniques, see the questioning book in this series.

Increasing the level of challenge is the theme of Chapter Eight. We look at some of the simplest techniques any teaching assistant can use to make the learning a bit more difficult. These techniques are most appropriate when learners are finding the work they have been set relatively easy. Here, we explore some of the ways you can help them to make better progress by ensuring a greater level of challenge.

Chapter Nine concentrates on memorisation techniques, acknowledging the fact that many learners find retaining information tricky. We look at five techniques you can use to help learners improve their retention of information. This makes it easier for them to make progress and to effectively build on their learning at a later date.

Finally, in Chapter Ten, we bring everything to a conclusion and provide a handy, easy-to-access recap of the strategies and techniques outlined in the book.

Overall, you will find forty strategies and techniques you can use to build high quality differentiation into your day-to-day work. Taken as a whole, they represent a detailed starting point for ensuring personalisation and helping all learners to access the learning and make great progress.

Don't feel you need to do everything at once, though. Instead, read on and, as you go, pick out strategies and techniques you would like to try with your learners. Once you've selected a handful to get started with, give these a go and see what happens. As you get more familiar and more comfortable with using this first batch of differentiation tools, you can come back to the book and make another selection of strategies and techniques to try. Taking this approach means that, over time, you'll be able to develop your practice so it becomes more and more differentiated, giving your learners an increasingly personalised learning experience.

Chapter 2 – Essential Techniques for Personalising Learning

Differentiation means personalising learning. Personalising learning means finding ways for it to make sense for learners. Finding ways in which they can access the learning and make good progress. These five essential techniques give you a great starting point for making this happen. You can use them in almost any situation, with almost any learner.

Connecting to Prior Experience

Learners come to us with prior experience. They know things, understand things, remember things and can do things. Connecting learning to prior experience means helping them understand how the current learning connects to what they already know, understand, remember or can do. It means contextualising the current learning in light of their existing experience.

This matters because it gives learners a sense of meaning and lets them use their existing experience to engage with new learning. It is therefore an excellent way to make learning personalised and to help learners access the work the teacher has set.

You can connect the current learning to prior experience in a number or ways. For example, you might ask learners what they already know about a topic, what they can remember about it, or what they have learned about it in the past. Another option is to create a brainstorm with your learners. Write the title of the topic on a piece of paper, draw a circle around it and challenge your learners to think of as many things as possible they already know about which connect to it.

In some lessons, the learning will be sufficiently relevant for learners to make highly specific and tangible connections, though these will often need your prompting if they are to come to light.

For example, in a geography lesson looking at the water cycle, a teaching assistant might ask their learner a question such as: 'Do we live near any reservoirs?' or 'Where do we get our drinking water from?'

On the rare occasion that learners have absolutely no prior experience on which they can call to make sense of new learning, don't fear. You can make a virtue out of this by explaining to learners that, as the learning progresses, so they will have opportunities to create new experiences. In addition, it is highly likely that during the learning hitherto unseen connections will come to light.

Simplifying

As soon as we simplify something we remove some of its complexity. This makes it easier for learners to access. If you are working one-to-one with a learner, or with a small group of learners, and you feel they are struggling to access the work, ask yourself if there is anything you could simplify. If there is, step in and make it simpler. Then see if your learners are now in a position to make sense of the work. If they are, that's great. If they're not, ask yourself whether you could simplify things further.

For example, a teaching assistant working in a numeracy lesson might simplify a task so their learner has time to practice adding fractions which have the same denominator before later going on to practice adding fractions with different denominators.

Another example is a history lesson in which learners have been given five sources to analyse. A teaching assistant is working with a small group of learners who are struggling to complete this task. They step in and remove three of the sources then say: 'OK, let's try analysing these two sources first. Once we've got to grips with these, I'll bring in source number three and we'll take a look at that. We can then keep going until we've done all five.'

And a third example is a literacy lesson in which learners are trying to write an alternative ending for a story the class has been reading over the last few weeks. A teaching assistant is working one-to-one with a learner who doesn't know how to tackle this task without copying the original ending. The teaching assistant simplifies matters by asking the learner to imagine how the ending could be different if one character was changed. This simple starting point offers the learner a path into the work. After an initial discussion, the teaching assistant can then bring in other elements, making the exercise more challenging and slowly bringing it closer to the original task set by the teacher.

Breaking Learning Down

Another way to simplify learning is to break it down. This is where we divide a task into a series of smaller tasks, or steps, and then tackle each one in turn. The great advantage of this approach is that we can devote all our energy and attention to one thing at a time, instead of feeling overloaded by having to think about everything all at once.

For example, a learner might be struggling to get started on a design task set by the teacher. This task asks them to do a number of things, culminating in an advertising campaign 'selling' the learning they have done over the past few lessons.

A teaching assistant is working one-to-one with this learner. Initially, they hold back. They want to give their learner every chance to be independent and to tackle the task on their own. After a couple of minutes, however, it becomes apparent that the learner is struggling to do this. So, the teaching assistant steps in. They break the task down into a series of five separate tasks. For example:

1) Make a list of all the things we've learned about in the past three lessons.

2) Decide which of these things you think are most important.

3) Choose three different things to include in your advertising campaign. For example, a TV advert, a radio advert and a poster.

4) Decide which part of the learning you want each of your advertising elements to focus on.

5) Plan your advertising elements and get started on making them.

Notice how these are the kind of steps many learners would go through automatically when faced with a task of this nature. The key here is that, for whatever reason, our learner doesn't have the means to break the learning down on their own. This is where the teaching assistant steps in. By breaking down the learning for the learner they provide them with a list of separate smaller tasks they can tackle one at a time. This means they can access the learning and complete the task.

Attaching Meaning to Learning

Meaning is key to motivation. When students don't understand why they are doing something or fail to see the reason behind what the teacher is asking them to do, motivation can sag, or disappear completely.

Sometimes, questions such as 'What's the point?' or 'When will I ever need to use this?' can be seen in a negative light, leading to negative responses. A classic scenario sees the learner expressing their frustration in this way, with the teacher responding dismissively because they perceive a slight implicit to the learner's comments.

Another familiar scenario is when a learner's questions are brushed aside or ignored. The reasoning behind this is that the questions are distractions or are intended to put off having to start the work. While this may be true, I think a better option is open to us.

Every part of the curriculum is there for a reason. Every part has been chosen because it is deemed important, relevant, useful or of intrinsic value. So, why not explain this to learners? Why not show them that all the learning they do has meaning? That it is inherently meaningful when viewed from the right perspective.

Two points follow. First, if your learners are struggling to access the work because they see no point to it and have low motivation as a result, explain to them why the learning matters – both in terms of their own development and in the context of wider society. For example, trigonometry helps learners to develop their analytical thinking, problem-solving skills and logical thinking. It is also a key feature of mathematics which, once grasped, let's you develop further expertise. In the wider world, trigonometry is used for a whole range of purposes in disciplines such as chemistry, physics and engineering. And, of course, you can use trigonometry to work out the shortest route home from school if you have three points to work with – simply follow the hypotenuse!

Second, look for ways to help learners attach meaning to the learning they do in lessons. Connect it to their goals, their targets and their development as a learner, thinker and young person. Link it to the wider world and the local community. And show how learners can use it in their own lives and to make sense of their own experiences.

All of this helps raise motivation and encourages learners to engage more positively with their learning.

Creating Opportunities for Success

At the start of a lesson or task, see if you can create opportunities for learners to experience success. This binds learners into the learning, giving them a positive experience with which to begin what they are doing. It also gives them a sense of achievement and sets them up to tackle whatever comes next.

The point here is not to provide learners with easy wins all the time. Instead, it is to help learners get into a topic or task by having them experience success in the early stages. This is likely to increase motivation and help learners feel they can be successful in their endeavours.

This technique is perhaps most useful when you are working with a learner who is low on confidence. Often, learners in this situation begin lessons or tasks with a fatalistic sense that they will not be successful, no matter what they do. These negative predictions are the result of past experiences and, perhaps more crucially, the perceptions learners have about themselves.

A learner who is low on confidence is less likely to feel they can be successful with their learning. They are more likely to foresee difficulties, problems and obstacles which will stop them (once again) from achieving what they want to achieve.

Creating opportunities for success early in a lesson or task means learners experience something which contrasts with these beliefs. It suggests an alternative to them, implying that they might be able to succeed. As such, it builds confidence, counterbalances negative thoughts and makes it easier for learners to access the learning and feel motivated to do so.

Here are five simple ways you can create opportunities for learners to experience success:

- Ask them to list all the things they know which are connected to the topic

- Challenge them to interview three people in the class and find out what they know or think about the topic

- Challenge them to come up with three questions they would like to ask about the topic – and then see if you can answer these together

- Invite them to ask you three questions about the topic and to then give you feedback on your answers

- Invite them to brainstorm all the things they can think of which connect to the task

Summary

In this chapter we've looked at five essential techniques you can use to personalise learning. These are:

- Connecting learning to learners' prior experience

- Simplifying

- Breaking learning down

- Attaching meaning to learning

- Creating opportunities for learners to experience success

Chapter 3 – Verbalising Thinking

Most learners are better speakers than writers. Speech is a natural function of the human body whereas writing is a technology. A cultural tool that is passed down through time and has to be learned in a different way. Nearly all the learners we work with can use speech to make sense of the learning we ask them to do. They can talk about ideas and information – to themselves, a partner, the whole class, their teacher, or a teaching assistant.

When we verbalise thinking, we have an opportunity to order, refine and edit our thoughts. We can also reflect on them and think about whether we want to change them or keep them as they are. Speaking can also be a form of practice. For example, when a learner speaks about their thinking they are also practising that thinking in a way that reinforces their understanding and memorisation of it.

All of this means that we can use techniques in which verbalising thinking is to the fore to help learners access learning and engage with the lesson content. These five techniques illustrate that fact:

Verbalising Your Thinking

You are an expert. You have knowledge and understanding in advance of the learners you work with. Your role in the classroom is to help and support your learners and you would not be there if you weren't in a position to do this. Verbalising your thinking means giving learners access to a model of how to think. They can then copy this model, borrow from it or imitate it.

For example, in a numeracy lesson looking at long division, a teaching assistant might be working with a learner who is struggling to get to grips with the work the teacher has set. The teaching assistant decides to walk the learner through how to do long division, verbalising their thinking as they go.

This means the learner gains access to the teaching assistant's expertise in how to do long division. This expertise is locked up in the teaching assistant's mind. By verbalising their thinking they make it accessible to the learner. The learner can then copy it, imitate or borrow from it.

In this particular example, we can imagine the teaching assistant walking their learner through the process of long division, verbalising their thinking as they go. They would probably do this slowly, at first. And they would probably draw their learner's attention to different elements of their thinking.

After they've done this, they invite their learner to have a go at one of the long division problems the teacher has set. They ask the learner to verbalise their own thinking as they go – and to copy the teaching assistant's thinking if they feel it will help.

You can apply this technique in all manner of contexts. Once learner's have access to your expert thinking they are better placed to access the learning. In addition, once they become familiar with how you verbalise your thinking, they will find it easier to do this for themselves. The benefits are twofold. First, it helps the learner to keep track of their own thinking, edit it and refine it. Second, it gives you a chance to assess learner thinking and step in if anything goes awry.

Discussing Tasks

Imagine this situation. The teacher has introduced the lesson. Learners have completed a starter activity and are generally engaged with the learning. The teacher, happy with how things are progressing, increases the level of challenge by introducing a new task, one intended to take up most of the rest of the lesson. This task has different elements to it, involves quite a lot of student self-direction and gets increasingly challenging as learners move through it.

You are working with a small group of learners the teacher has identified as needing additional support. They see the task displayed on the board, hear the teacher's explanation and feel overwhelmed. How, they think, can we make sense of this, let alone complete it?

This is a perfect opportunity for you to lead your learners in a discussion of the task. Why? Because discussing the task will help them to make sense of it. Verbalising their thinking about the task will help make that thinking clearer and will give them a chance to both share their uncertainties and talk through what they think they don't understand.

So, you say the following: 'Turn to your partner and ask them what they think we need to do first.' After twenty seconds or so, call the learners back and ask them to share their thoughts. This is the starting point of your discussion. You can move things on by using questions such as:

- How would you break the task down into three parts?

- What do you think will be the easiest part of the task? What about the hardest?

- How could we tackle the task? What could we use that we already know?

- How will we know if we have been successful with the task?

- What difficulties or challenges might there be in the task? How could we overcome these?

All of this gives learners a chance to analyse the task, talk through their thinking, and gain a better understanding of both what the task entails and how to engage with it.

Discussing Questions

We can apply the same principle to the discussion of questions. If learners are faced with a question they are struggling to access, then we can help them to make sense of it by engaging them in a discussion which lets them verbalise their thinking.

For example, a religious studies lesson might see the teacher pose a question such as the following: 'Is it ever right to forgive people who have done bad things?'

You might be working with a learner who takes one look at that question and draws a blank. They are not sure how to answer and decide to take a safety-first route. This means withdrawing from the question and not risking any answer whatsoever.

At this point, you step in and begin to discuss the question with your learner. This gives them a chance to verbalise their thinking and let's you take them through a series of steps which makes it easier for them to access the learning. It might look something like this:

Teaching Assistant: What are your first thoughts about the question?

Learner: I don't know.

Teaching Assistant: OK, let's try breaking the question down. What does forgiveness mean?

Learner: It means when you forgive someone for something they've done. So, like, you're saying that what they did wasn't good but you can put it to one side and move on from it.

Teaching Assistant: Have you ever forgiven anyone?

Learner: Yeah, of course. Me and my brother fight all the time. But we don't really mean it so we forgive each other afterwards and just forget about it.

Teaching Assistant: Do you think there are some times when it isn't possible to forgive?

Learner: Well, yeah, I guess there must be. Like if people do really bad things. Crimes and things like that. Then it's much harder to forgive people because they might have wrecked someone's life and that's a bit different from me fighting with my brother.

Teaching Assistant: So, do you think there could be different types of forgiveness?

Learner: Um, maybe. Maybe you forgive people more easily if you're really close to them and if what they've done isn't that serious.

Notice how, in this discussion, the teaching assistant uses a series of questions to help the learner verbalise their thinking. Each question is simpler than the first question posed by the teacher. Each one helps the learner to think about a different part of the initial question. By the end of the discussion, the learner has verbalised their thinking to such an extent that they are able to answer the initial question and, therefore, access the learning.

Discussing Strategies

A third area on which you can focus discussion is that of strategies. These are the things learners use to tackle their learning. Strategies include:

1) Trial and error – give things a go and then make adjustments

2) Making mistakes and seeing what happens – use your mistakes to help you learn

3) Asking questions – use questions to find out more information

4) Dividing things up – try doing one thing at a time

5) Using feedback – this can help you to change your approach

6) Practice – when you practice, you get more familiar with the challenge

7) Ask yourself what it's like – is it like anything you've seen or done before?

We use strategies all the time when we're trying to solve problems, support our learners and successfully complete our work. Many students struggle to think about strategies, though. They may not feel confident to apply different strategies in different situations. Or, they may struggle to identify different strategies they can use.

Discussing strategies means helping learners verbalise their thinking on how to tackle tasks. It also means prompting them to think and talk about different ways in which they can go about accessing the learning. Here's an example of such a discussion:

Teaching Assistant: How could we try to tackle this task?

Learner: I don't know.

Teaching Assistant: What did we do the last time we were stuck?

Learner: Um, we tried splitting the text up into three different bits. Then we looked at one bit at a time instead of trying to do it all at once.

Teaching Assistant: Do you think that could work this time?

Learner: Yeah, I guess it could.

Teaching Assistant: Let's have a look at this, then. How would you divide this piece of writing into three?

Learner: OK, well this bit is definitely the introduction because the journalist is setting the scene and telling you about where they are, who's involved and all those things.

Teaching Assistant: I agree. And you've used your knowledge of what makes an introduction to identify that. Well done. Now, where would you make the next split?

Learner: Well, I think we probably need to find the conclusion and split that off. Then we have an introduction, a middle and a conclusion. And we can look at each bit separately.

In this example, the teaching assistant uses the discussion to help the learner talk through a strategy they can use to complete the task (in this case, analysing a newspaper article). The discussion is an opportunity for the learner to verbalise their ideas, reflect on them and to also think back to a strategy they have successfully used in the past. This again demonstrates how helping learners to verbalise their thinking can help them to access the learning.

Using Discussion to Precede Writing

Our final technique in this chapter involves using discussion to precede writing. If you have a learner who finds writing difficult, or who is reluctant to get started with their writing, this technique is a really good way to help them experience success.

As we've noted already, we can use speech to order, refine and edit our thinking. In addition, most learners are better speakers than writers. It follows, therefore, that we can get our learners to use their strengths to their own benefit.

Imagine we have a learner who is struggling to get started on a history essay. The teaching assistant is circulating through the history class, working in tandem with the teacher to offer support and guidance to all the learners who need it.

The teaching assistant pulls up a chair and starts talking to the learner about their essay. They use techniques similar to those outlined in the last three entries to draw out the learner's thinking. Through this, they help them to verbalise their ideas, their thoughts about how to tackle the essay, as well as their uncertainties about what to do.

The teaching assistant might use questions such as the following:

- What is the most important thing you think you need to write about?

- What would be a good first sentence to get the reader interested?

- How could you include some of the sources we've looked at?

- How will you make sure you answer the question in every paragraph?

- What three things should you definitely include in your essay?

Through the discussion, the learner has a chance to articulate their thoughts about the essay. They are coming up with a plan they can use – getting their ideas in order, ready to begin. When the discussion is over, the learner is primed and ready to go. The essay no longer feels hard to start, monolithic or inaccessible. The verbalisation of thinking has put paid to that.

You can adapt this technique for any situation in which learners need to write. Simply engage them in discussion before they start trying to write. This makes it easier for them to start writing, and to sustain their writing as well.

Summary

In this chapter we've looked at five strategies connected to verbalising thinking, all of which you can use to help learners access the learning. These are:

- Verbalising your thinking, giving learners access to your expertise

- Discussing tasks with learners

- Discussing questions with learners

- Discussing strategies with learners

- Using discussion to precede writing

Chapter 4 – Approaches to Explanation

Explanation aids understanding. If learners don't understand things during a lesson, we may need to use additional explanation to help them access the learning. This explanation supplements that provided by the teacher. There are lots of different ways we can explain ideas and information. Having a collection of explanation strategies on hand means you are well-prepared to support learners who are struggling. Here are five key strategies:

Images

Images provide learners with access to visual information, and this information takes a markedly different form to information which is verbal or written (though don't forget that writing is a special form of visual communication).

We can use images to help explain ideas and information to our learners. They are particularly useful as a supplement to verbal explanation. For example, you might find yourself in a science lesson about volcanoes. The teacher explains to the class how volcanoes are formed and then sets learners off on a fact-finding research mission.

You are working with a pair of learners who find science difficult. They listened carefully to the teacher's explanation but are clearly still somewhat uncertain over how volcanoes form. At this point, you recognise that they are struggling to access the learning. Asking them to go on a fact-finding mission might help matters – but it also might compound their difficulties, because they will be engaging with the lesson content while still uncertain about the central idea.

So, you decide to step in and explain the idea a second time. You have a tablet computer provided by the school and you use this to bring up a series of images related to how volcanoes form. As you repeat the explanation given by the teacher, you supplement this verbal information with the visual information contained in the images.

Two points follow. First, learners get two bites at the cherry. They can try to make sense of the verbal explanation and they can also try to make sense of the visual explanation provided through the images. Second, learners can cross-check their understanding. They can see if the pictures match up with what they have interpreted the words to mean. This helps them to feel more certain about how they've interpreted the words. It also gives them an opportunity to reflect on whether their understanding of the words feels right or not. If there is a big disconnect with the images, then something remains amiss. If the two tally, however, all is likely to be well.

Re-explaining

When it comes to explaining, we can't always assume that once is enough. We may need to re-explain ideas or information to our learners two or three times, depending on the circumstances.

For example, we might be working with a learner who has a negative attitude towards maths. Whenever anything new is introduced in their maths lessons, their immediate reaction is to withdraw and say they don't understand it. In this situation, we will probably need to re-explain new ideas two, three or even four times, in an effort to engage the learner and help them to access the work – by getting over their initial response.

There are various different ways in which you can re-explain.

One is to make each explanation simpler than the last. For example, a teaching assistant might be re-explaining gravity to a learner who is encountering the concept in a science lesson for the first time. They begin by repeating the teacher's explanation. Then, they simplify this, using simpler language and familiar examples. They then explain gravity for a third time, using even simpler language and accompanying this with a visual demonstration (dropping a pen onto the desk from head height).

Another technique is to use a series of different examples. For example, a teaching assistant might be re-explaining onomatopoeia to a learner in an English lesson. They do this three times, using a different example on each occasion. This quickly builds up a small set of reference points in the learner's mind, helping them to make sense of the term.

A third technique is to re-explain an idea or information three times, using more specific examples on each occasion. The idea here is that you help learners to build up a more detailed understanding of the idea or information in question because they are able to start developing a mental map of how it applies in different settings. For example, a teaching assistant might re-explain the idea of translation in maths by first using a general example, then the example of a single shape, then the example of three different shapes.

Stories

Stories helps us make sense of the world. When we make a new acquaintance, we might give them a brief story to explain who we are. When we get home from work, we might tell our partner the story of our day. When we are young, we hear and read stories which tell us about the world – about things like right and wrong, how to act, different ways to think and what to do if things don't go our way.

Two of the most famous examples of stories as explanations are Aesop's Fables and Jesus' Parables. In both these examples, stories are used to help people understand abstract ideas. For example, in Aesop's fable 'The Hare and The Tortoise' the story serves as a vessel through which to explain and communicate ideas around persistence, effort and arrogance, among other things.

You can use stories to explain ideas and information to your learners. They will be familiar with stories – with how they work, how they are structured and what they contain – and you can use this familiarity to yours and their advantage. Here are three examples of how you might use stories as part of your explanations, to help learners access the learning:

- If you want to explain values or ways of behaving to learners, try using a fable, parable or other similar story. For example, you might use the story of the tortoise and the hare to help learners understand why persistence matters.

- Find stories connected to new topics learners are going to cover. For example, if learners are studying gravity in their science lessons, read up on the story of how Isaac Newton discovered gravity and use this to explain the idea to your learners.

- Help learners understand previous lessons by retelling them as a story. For example, if you are working one-to-one with a learner and they are struggling to make sense of the learning, try retelling the previous lesson as a story – with a beginning, a middle and an end. This will help reactivate the learner's existing knowledge and understanding. You can then ask them how they could apply it to the current learning.

Examples

Examples give learners something concrete they can hang onto. They help learners build up a mental map of what a certain idea or piece of information means. Without examples, ideas can remain abstract. For many learners, this can make life difficult.

Using examples when you explain things means giving learners lots of different ways through which to make sense of your explanations and, by extension, to access the learning. You can use examples to demonstrate, illustrate and exemplify.

When giving examples, think about using ones learners are already familiar with. This means you tap into their prior experience, knowledge and understanding (as per the entry in Chapter Two). Doing this makes it easier for learners to assimilate new ideas and information. They can fit them into their existing frames of reference and use their existing knowledge and understanding to make sense of the new learning.

Another option is to use a range of examples. Here, two paths are open to you. First, you might give a series of similar examples, using these to help learners understand your explanation by seeing it from a number of different, but closely connected, viewpoints. For example, in a maths lesson, a teaching assistant might help a learner to understand the difference between acute and obtuse angles by giving them five examples of each. This helps remove uncertainty and lets the learner feel confident that by grasping one or two examples, they are really grasping all of them.

Second, you might give a series of different examples. This is relevant if the idea or information you are explaining can be illustrated in a number of different ways. In our previous example, we used acute and obtuse angles. While there are many of both, they are all essentially the same. However, if we were explaining persuasive writing to a learner, we might use examples from a newspaper, a TV advert, a company brochure, a speech and a website. The purpose would be to help the learner understand the explanation, but also to appreciate the range of situations to which the explanation relates.

However you choose to use examples, remember that they give learners a way to make sense of abstract or general ideas and information.

Analogies

Neutrons and protons inside an atomic nucleus are packed together like sweets in a jar. Electrons move around the nucleus like the planets orbiting the sun. Splitting an atom releases a huge amount of energy, like a volcanic eruption.

These three sentences demonstrate the strengths and limitations of using analogies to help explain ideas and information to learners.

First, the strengths.

Analogies are often vivid and evocative. In each of the examples above, the analogy conjures up a clear image. One that is likely to stay in the mind. Analogies make use of things we already know. In the examples above, our learners already know about sweets in a jar, the solar system, and volcanoes. We use this existing knowledge to help learners make sense of new knowledge. We compare new with old, as a way to bridge the gape between what we do know and what we don't yet know. And analogies can be easily formed around everyday examples that are familiar to learners. This means we can again make use of prior experience as a route into helping learners understand new information and ideas.

Now, the weaknesses.

Electrons move around an atomic nucleus like planets orbiting the sun. It is not an exact match. Just a similarity. We must be careful to ensure that learners don't think both parts of an analogy are exactly the same. Some analogies might be slightly off-beam. The nucleus of an atom is not really that close to sweets packed into a jar. We need to make sure the analogy is fit for purpose before we use it. And some analogies might give learners the wrong impression. Splitting the atom releases a lot of energy, but the scale of an atom is totally different to the scale of a volcano.

Overall, analogies are too good an explanation tool to ignore. They offer learners vivid, easily accessible explanations connected to their existing knowledge and understanding. As a result, we can use them to help learners get to grips with ideas and information they are struggling to understand. Analogies can be an excellent way to help learners access the learning. But, we must also be mindful when using them that they are not without their risks. A careful and judicious approach usually works best.

Summary

In this chapter we've looked at five different approaches to explanation. These are:

- Using images to supplement verbal explanation and as an alternative source of explanation

- Re-explaining ideas and information to learners

- Using stories

- Giving examples

- Using analogies

Chapter 5 – Scaffolding Strategies

Scaffolding is when we do a little bit of the work for the learner, making life that bit easier for them. They are then in a position to start the work and to access the learning on their own. For example, a teaching assistant working with a learner in a literacy lesson could scaffold the work for them by providing sentence starters. The learner could use these to get going with their writing. The sentence starters do a little bit of the work for the learner, leaving them to then do the rest.

Another example would be a teaching assistant working with a learner in a food technology lesson. The learner might struggle to follow instructions and so the teaching assistant rewrites the original recipe provided by the teacher so it is simpler. The learner can use this revised recipe to access the work. Again, the teaching assistant does a little bit of the work for the learner (in this case, synthesising the information contained in the recipe), making the learning more accessible for them.

With those thoughts in mind, here are five scaffolding strategies you can use to differentiate learning in almost any setting:

Memory Extensions

Working memory is limited to seven pieces of information, plus or minus two, for the vast majority of the population. Working memory is short-term memory.

The memory we use to process information in the moment. If this memory gets overloaded, learners can feel like they are struggling to get anywhere. They may withdraw as a result, or decide the work is too hard for them to complete.

As soon as we remove information from our working memory, we free up space. One way to think about this is that we can expand our working memory if we write things down. A piece of scrap paper becomes an extension of our working memory. A mini-whiteboard extends our memory beyond the limitations of our brain.

This is a wonderful strategy we can help all learners to use. We can show them how to extend the capacity of their working memories.

For example, we might have a learner who is trying to do a difficult maths sum in their head. They keep coming up against a block and, after a few attempts, they give up. We step in and hand them a piece of scrap paper. 'Use this,' we say. 'Take some of the information out of your mind and store it on the paper.' Suddenly, they can solve the sum. They have freed up space in their working memory by using the paper and no longer feel overloaded.

Another example is a learner in a literacy lesson who is struggling to write a poem. We hand them a mini-whiteboard and say: 'Write all the words down you want to include, then cross off each one as you get it into your poem.' The same thing happens. Suddenly the task becomes easier. They can store their key ideas on the whiteboard and devote their working memory to coming up with lines for the poem.

Memory extensions like scrap paper and mini-whiteboards scaffold learning by doing a bit of the short-term remembering for learners. They can then focus their efforts on other matters, avoid overload and successfully access the learning.

Classroom Tools

Classrooms are littered with tools learners can use to scaffold their own learning. Drawing learners' attention to these tools means helping them to remain independent and take charge of their own learning. Here are some examples of classroom tools:

- Dictionaries

- Thesauruses

- Word charts

- Wall displays

- Maps

- Atlases

- Posters containing grammatical rules

- Lists of nouns, verbs or conjunctions

- Times table posters

Learners can use all of these to help themselves access learning. For example, we might have a learner in a geography lesson who is struggling to identify why people might choose to migrate from rural to urban areas. They don't yet have sufficient knowledge and understanding to explain why this happens.

On trying and failing to come up with an answer, the learner gets despondent. A teaching assistant is working with the class, circulating through the room and helping learners who need support. They spot this learner, go over and talk to them about what's happened. On hearing the learner's version of events, they suggest getting an atlas and comparing a map of London with a map of rural Northumberland. This, they suggest, might help the learner to identify some reasons behind rural to urban migration.

In this example we see a few things. First, the teaching assistant is aware of the classroom tools available to learners. Second, the teaching assistant understands that scaffolding doesn't have to involve them doing something for the learner to make the learning a little easier. It can also involve them helping the learner to understand how they can scaffold their own learning (the atlas does some of the work for the learner by presenting the differences between urban and rural areas, they then have to interpret this). Third, the learner is able to scaffold their own learning by using a tool. Although, if they still find themselves in difficulty, the teaching assistant can step in and offer further support.

Over time, you can train learners to use classroom tools themselves, without needing you to prompt them. This encourages independence and helps learners to personalise their own learning.

Starting Learners Off

If you are working with a learner who is struggling to get started then take the initiative and start them off yourself. This means doing a little bit of the work for them, before handing things over and inviting them to carry on.

Sometimes, learners can feel overwhelmed at having to start a piece of work. This feeling tends to come from one of two places. Either the learner lacks confidence and feels they don't have the means to start the work, or the learner sees so many different possibilities for starting things off that they feel swamped by choice and find it easier to withdraw then make a decision.

In either case, your intervention speeds up the process, meaning the learner can spend more time and energy on engaging with the learning.

For example, we might have a numeracy lesson in which the teacher has set their learners a challenge. They have to choose five worksheets from a selection of eight and complete these within the lesson. All the worksheets are connected to shape and some are more challenging than others.

A teaching assistant is working one-to-one with a learner. The learner has no problem selecting their first sheet, but then they find themselves uncertain about how to start. There are five problems on the sheet, but these aren't numbered. The learner looks at one, goes to begin, pulls back, then turns to a second and repeats the action. At this point, the teaching assistant steps in, numbers the problems one to five and then invites the learner to begin at number one. This simple intervention helps the learner get started and, in so doing, makes it easier for them to access the work.

Another example is a sociology lesson in which learners are writing essays. A teaching assistant is working with a group of three learners who struggle with writing and need extra support in this area. Writing an essay is a big thing for these learners. They feel overwhelmed and this expresses itself as an inability to get started. The teaching assistant intervenes and suggests an opening sentence. The learners write this down and quickly find themselves in a position from which they can move off and continue writing. The little bit of scaffolding provided by the teaching assistant makes it easier for all the learners to access the learning.

Suggesting Options

Another technique you can use if learners are struggling to get started is to suggest options. For example:

Learner: I'm not sure what to do. I don't think I can do this.

Teaching Assistant: Well, let's have a look at this together. OK, how about this. You could either start by explaining what you think about the picture, or you could start by explaining what the picture looks like. Which do you think is the best option?

In this example, the teaching assistant scaffolds the learning by giving their learner two possible ways in which to get started. This means the learner retains a degree of independence. After all, they have to make a choice about which option to go for. At the same time, it helps the learner achieve what they are struggling to achieve on their own – getting started.

You can use this technique whenever learners are uncertain about how to begin a piece of work. Generally speaking, two or three options are sufficient. Any more than this and it becomes harder for the learner to hold the options in their mind and discriminate between them.

The technique can also be used to scaffold learning during activities, or when learners are struggling to answer a question. In the first case, we might imagine that a learner has been successfully engaging with a task but then hits a point at which the level of challenge increases quite sharply. They experience an abrupt change in how they are getting on with the learning, prompting them to slow down and maybe grind to a halt. If this happens, the teaching assistant can step in, assess what has caused the problem and then present a set of options in exactly the same manner as outlined above.

In the second case, if you find one of your learners is struggling to respond to a question – posed by you or by the teacher – then try presenting them with two or three possible answers from which to select. These options scaffold the learner's interaction with the question. They no longer have to identify an answer from the myriad potential answers out there. Instead, they have to choose one from a small set of options. Again, this scaffolds the learning, making it easier for them to access it and engage with the lesson.

Prompting and Clueing

Our final scaffolding technique is a combination of two complementary strategies – prompting and clueing. Prompting is when we prompt learners to think back to something they already know about and can use in the current situation. Clueing is when we give learners a clue that can help them to access the learning. Let's look at an example of each, to illustrate the difference. First, prompting:

Teaching Assistant: What might be the best way to tackle the task?

Learner: I don't know…I'm not sure…

Teaching Assistant: Didn't we have a task like this last week? On Thursday, I think.

Learner: Hmmm, did we?

Teaching Assistant: I think it might have been after breaktime…

Learner: Oh, yes. I remember. We did do something similar. Do you think I could use the same approach on this task?

Now, clueing:

Teaching Assistant: What might be the best way to tackle the task?

Learner: I don't know...I'm not sure...

Teaching Assistant: Maybe the answer is on Page 32 of the textbook?

Learner: Page 32? Let me have a look...

In the first example, the teaching assistant prompts the learner to think about something they already know and understand. They prompt them to remember what they did previously and to apply this to the current situation. In the second example, the teaching assistant gives the learner a clue. This clue points them in the direction of an answer. The answer in this case being about how to tackle the task.

Both prompting and clueing are examples of scaffolding. Both do a little bit of work for the learner, but then leave them to do the rest on their own. Prompting sees a higher level of independence than clueing. In prompting, the teaching assistant is sending the learner back to something they already know or can do but have forgotten about. In clueing, the level of independence is slightly lower. The teaching assistant is sending the learner to something they are not yet familiar with but which will help them to access the learning.

Both tools are worth using on a regular basis – the situation will determine whether you think prompting or clueing is most appropriate. Though don't forget that if you start with prompting you can always move on to clueing, whereas the reverse isn't usually the case.

Summary

In this chapter we've focussed on scaffolding. The five scaffolding techniques we've examined are:

- Helping learners to use memory extensions such as scrap paper and mini-whiteboards

- Helping learners to use a variety of classroom tools

- Starting learners off with their work

- Suggesting options from which learners can choose

- Using prompting and clueing to help learners access the learning

Chapter 6 – Modelling Techniques

Modelling is the process whereby we show learners what we want them to do. Our demonstration provides them with a model they can copy, imitate or borrow from. Modelling is particularly good if learners are meeting something for the first time, if they need really clear guidance on how to do something, or if you feel they are continuing to struggle after you have offered other forms of support.

You can model a whole range of things for your learners. For example, you might model how to think about a problem, how to write a sentence, how to analyse a poem, how to play a pass in football or how to follow a recipe in a food technology lesson. In each case, your modelling gives learners a way into the learning. In the rest of this chapter we'll look at five specific modelling strategies in greater depth.

Modelling Thinking

Modelling thinking means showing learners how to think about a topic, a problem, an idea or some information. For example, a teaching assistant might be working one-to-one with a learner in a numeracy lesson. The learner is struggling to complete their work successfully and so the teaching assistant models how to think about certain sums and mathematical processes. By doing this, they give the learner a starting point for changing their own thinking.

Modelling thinking gives access to your expertise as a thinker. Learners can borrow from this, using it to change, refine and improve their own thinking.

Another example might be a teaching assistant working one-to-one with a learner in a literacy lesson. This learner is struggling to write coherent paragraphs. To help, the teaching assistant models how to construct a paragraph. They talk the learner through their thinking as they go, giving them access to their expertise. After they've done this, they invite the learner to try again. The learner can now attempt to copy the model the teaching assistant has provided, or borrow bits from it, and therefore change their own thinking about how to construct a paragraph.

When modelling thinking, make sure your learner understands what you are doing. Draw their attention to the process by saying something like: 'OK, let me show you one way to think about. Have a listen to my thinking and see if you can think in that way as well.'

A comment like this directs the learner's attention towards what you are doing. It primes them to listen out for the modelling of thinking and to think about how they would subsequently use what they hear to adapt their own efforts.

A final point to note is that when you first start modelling thinking for your learners you may need to slow things down a touch. This helps them to get on board with what you are doing and makes it easier for them to access your modelling. Over time, as learners become familiar with this approach, you can speed up.

Modelling Strategy Selection

Imagine we have a learner who hits an obstacle in their work and decides to give up as a result. They don't believe there is any way past the obstacle. They take it as an end point – as confirmation that they have reached their limit. They withdraw and, as a consequence, are no longer accessing the learning.

Modelling strategy selection is one way you can help learners overcome such situations. This means showing them how to identify and apply a strategy when faced with a difficulty, obstacle or problem. It means giving them a model they can use whenever they are faced with one of these situations. Here's an example of what it might look like in practice:

Teaching Assistant: What could you try next?

Learner: I don't know. I don't think I can do any more.

Teaching Assistant: OK, well, why don't we try thinking about how to choose a strategy?

Learner: What does that mean?

Teaching Assistant: A strategy is how you try to approach a problem. A method you use to get past an obstacle.

Learner: Maybe that could work...

Teaching Assistant: So, I'm looking at the problem and I'm thinking to myself, 'What strategies do I know about and could I use them here?' Now, I know that trial and error is often a good strategy, and I know that breaking things down is a good one as well. So how about I try breaking the problem down into a couple of different parts and then try using trial and error on each one to look for a solution. What do you think?

Learner: Yeah, that might be a good plan.

In this example the teaching assistant presents the learner with a model of how to think about strategy selection. They show the learner what to do, taking them through the necessary steps. The learner is then in a position to copy, imitate or borrow from this approach in the future.

Model Sentences

We know some learners we work with struggle with writing. They may find it difficult or experience negative emotions when faced with a writing task. One option they might opt for is to withdraw from the task. Another option is to find ways of avoiding writing tasks. However, we also know that they need to practice writing if they are to get better at it. We therefore want to find ways through which we can engage them with writing and help them to access the learning.

Model sentences are one technique we can call on to help. This is where we provide learners with examples of what good sentences look like, examples they can use as the basis of their own writing.

For example, you might be working with a learner in a science lesson, helping them to write up an experiment they have just done. This learner enjoyed completing the experiment but is now experiencing negative emotions provoked by their dislike of writing. This causes them to try a variety of avoidance tactics. In short, they are putting off getting started.

You decide to support the learner by coming up with a series of model sentences, one for each of the sections of the write-up. The learner can then use these to begin each part of their write-up. Rather than just write these sentences down, though, you talk the learner through the thought processes underpinning your writing.

First, you show them how you identified each of the different sections needed in the write-up. Then, you explain how you selected a focus for each of the sentences. Finally, you talk them through how you constructed each sentence. This is doubly beneficial for the learner. They end up with a series of model sentences they can use to get started on their writing and they have had a chance to listen to you explaining how you go about sentence construction. They can copy, imitate or borrow from your model sentences as they move forward with their work. And they can do the same with the model thinking to which you gave them access.

Exemplar Work

Exemplar work is work which shows learners how to do something to a good standard. For example, if learners are writing an essay, we might show them a successful essay written by a learner who was in the class last year. Or, if learners are in a PE lesson trying to make long passes in rugby, we might show them a video of a learner doing this successfully in a lesson the previous week.

Exemplar work gives learners a complete model they can use to make sense of learning, to understand what good looks like, and from which they can borrow elements to include in their own work.

For example, a learner who is given access to the exemplar essay might borrow some of the approaches used by the original author. We would not want them to copy what their peer did, but we would want them to use in their own work some of the ideas and approaches exemplified through the essay.

In the rugby example, we might find a group of learners watching the video on a tablet computer. They would then try to imitate what they had seen. Their effort would be directed towards recreating the successful long passing demonstrated on the video.

In both of these examples we see the power of exemplar work. It gives learners something to aim for, something to borrow from, and something to use as a reference point for their own work. It is a model of what good looks like. Over time, learners can internalise such models until they reach a point at which they implicitly understand what good looks like and no longer need the external reference point.

So, how can you use exemplar work with your learners? Three specific approaches immediately come to mind:

1) Borrow work from learners who are successfully engaging with the learning and use this as a model from which other learners can borrow.

2) Create exemplar work to use with your learners.

3) Ask the teacher you work with to collect exemplar work showcasing different skills, to photocopy this and to give it to you to use with your learners.

Modelling Positive Self-Talk

Some learners may struggle to access the learning because of low confidence, low self-esteem, or negative perceptions of what it is possible for them to achieve. Modelling positive self-talk means showing them how they can change their thinking. The idea is that if a learner views themselves and their potential in a more positive light, they are more likely to keep going, try harder and persist. Here's an example of what it might look like in practice:

Teaching Assistant: Do you think you could try again?

Learner: What's the point? I'll never get any better.

Teaching Assistant: Sometimes we all feel like that. But you can think differently about what's possible as well.

Learner: I doubt it.

Teaching Assistant: A good way to start is to remind yourself of what you've done already. So, you might say that even though this feels difficult, you know that you've been able to overcome challenges before. Like last week, when you wrote that really interesting story and read out a section of it to the rest of the class.

Learner: Uh-huh.

Teaching Assistant: Another good technique is to think about how you will feel when you overcome the challenge. You can use this as motivation. Then you can start thinking about what you need to do first to make some progress. What do you think?

Learner: Well, I guess I could give that a try.

Here, the teaching assistant models two examples of how to use positive self-talk. Neither example is about unequivocal back-slapping. Both focus on thinking reasonably and rationally about the situation. In both examples, the teaching assistant models for the learner how to change their way of thinking about a problem from negative to positive.

In the first example, the emphasis is on using past experiences as a reference point for future success. In the second example, the emphasis is on using future goals as a reference point for motivation in the present. Both techniques demonstrate how to flip self-talk from negative to positive.

Summary

In this chapter we've focussed on modelling. Here are the five techniques we've examined, all of which you can use to help learners access the learning:

- Modelling thinking so as to give learners access to your expertise

- Modelling strategy selection so learners understand how to use appropriate strategies

- Model sentences as a basis for learners to develop their own writing

- Exemplar work as a reference point from which learners can borrow

- Modelling positive self-talk so learners can change how they think and feel about themselves and their learning.

Chapter 7 – Differentiating Your Questions

We use questions all the time. They are one of the main ways we communicate with learners. In the classroom, we ask hundreds of questions every day. The topic of questioning is examined in detail in the questioning book which forms part of this series. For now, let us look at five simple strategies you can use to differentiate your questions in any lesson.

Concrete to Abstract

Imagine a line running from completely concrete at one end to completely abstract at the other. We can think of this line as a continuum. At the completely concrete end there are questions like: 'What colour is the table?' 'How much does the bag weigh?' and 'How many ducks are in the pond?' At the completely abstract end of the line there are questions like: 'What does it mean to be human?' 'Do we all perceive colour in the same way?' 'Is it possible to prove that time exists?'

Concrete questions are generally easier to answer than abstract ones. We can use this principle, along with the idea of the continuum, to differentiate our questions.

When working with learners in the classroom, try posing them more or less concrete questions depending on how easy they are finding the learning.

For example, a teaching assistant might be questioning a learner in a science lesson. To begin, they use a series of concrete questions. Ones that sit right at the concrete end of the continuum. The learner finds these questions easy to answer. So, the teaching assistant decides to make things a little bit more challenging. To do this, they start asking slightly more abstract questions.

They move along the continuum, slowly, towards the abstract end. This means the difficulty of the questions gradually increases. The teaching assistant keeps going until they notice that their learner is having to think really hard about their answers. Thus, an equilibrium has been found. The teaching assistant's questions have hit the right level of challenge, based on where the learner is currently at.

You can use the idea of concrete to abstract to underpin your questioning at any time during a lesson. And it works in reverse as well. If you find your learners struggling to answer your questions, try making them a bit more concrete.

Here's a set of questions ranging from highly concrete to highly abstract you can use as a reference point:

1) How many ducks are in the pond? **(Highly Concrete)**

2) What colour are the ducks?

3) How are the ducks behaving?

4) What are the relationships between the ducks?

5) What might be influencing the behaviour of the ducks?

6) Why might the ducks have come to be as they are?

7) Is all human life mirrored in the vagaries of ducks?

8) If ducks could speak, would we understand them? **(Highly Abstract)**

General to Specific

This is where your questions go from highly general to highly specific. The more specific your questions get the more precise learners have to be with their answers. You can use highly general questions to get learners thinking about a topic and accessing the learning. You can then use more specific questions to challenge them and stretch their thinking. Here's an example set of questions running from highly general to highly specific:

- What do you think about friendship? **(Highly General)**

- What makes a good friend?

- Are all friendships the same?

- When is a friendship most important?

- In what circumstances do you think you should be able to call on a friend?

- If a friend needed your help, how much help would you be prepared to give and why?

- Can you think of a specific scenario in which a friendship might be tested to the point of breaking?

- How would you explain the limits of friendship and the different things it is acceptable and unacceptable for friends to ask of one another? **(Highly Specific)**

Notice how the length and tenor of the questions changes as they becomes more specific. The last question asks the learner to think really carefully about the topic of friendship. They need to come up with a detailed, precise answer in response. On the other hand, the first question is highly general. The learner needs to think about it but there are few restrictions on their thinking. This is a much easier question to answer.

'General to specific' works in the same way as 'concrete to abstract'. We have a continuum running from one type of question to another. As we move along the continuum, so the questions get more challenging. You can use more or less specific questions to find the right level of challenge for your learners, personalising their interaction with the lesson content.

Show Me, Tell Me, Convince Me

A third questioning technique is 'Show Me, Tell Me, Convince Me'. This is a three-part strategy you can use to find the right level of challenge for your learners. Each element is more challenging than the last. Here's an example of how it works:

Teaching Assistant: Can you show me how the Vikings invaded Britain?

Learner: They came by boat. You can see on the map how they came across the sea.

Teaching Assistant: Can you tell me why they came by boat and why they decided to invade?

Learner: They were good sailors already and could make good boats they could use to sail between places. They decided to invade because they wanted to take over more lands and Britain looked like a nice place to live.

Teaching Assistant: Can you convince me there was nothing people in Britain could do to stop the Vikings once they invaded?

Learner: Hmm, let me think about that...

Each question posed by the teaching assistant is more challenging than the last. The learner first only has to show the teaching assistant something – a simple procedure. Then they have to explain, with this signified by the word 'tell'. This is a more complex procedure and so is more challenging. Finally, the learner has to convince the teaching assistant of something. This is more challenging again as it requires the use of argumentation and persuasive techniques.

There are lots of situations in which you can call on this questioning strategy. It is a good way to quickly increase the level of challenge for a learner you are working with one-to-one. As shown in the example, you can swiftly move from one level of questioning to the next, and do this in a natural, organic way.

If a learner gets stuck at a certain level, take this as evidence that you are hitting an appropriate level of challenge for them at that point in time. Pursue this by asking them more questions at that level. Help them to explore their thinking here before trying to push them on again with a new set of questions.

Helping Learners Develop Their Own Questions

Many learners find developing questions difficult. If we help learners to ask good questions, we also help them to access the learning. The questions they ask will be questions connected to the learning, meaning their questions are a function of them interacting with and accessing the lesson content.

Here are five techniques you can use to help learners develop their own questions:

1) Model Questions. This is where you give your learners one or more model questions they can use as a guide for what makes a good question. For example, a teaching assistant working in a literacy lesson might write down three or four model questions about the work and give these to the learner they are working with. The learner can then use these as a starting point for coming up with their own questions.

2) Question Stems. Question stems are the beginning bits of questions. Like 'What if...' 'How might...' and 'Do you think...' Providing learners with a range of question stems means giving them a selection of different ways in which to start their questions. This is a form of scaffolding, making it easier for them to develop their own questions.

3) 5Ws and 1H. As in: Who, What, Where, When, Why and How? This is a classic question you can share with your learners. Once they are familiar with it they can use it as a framework for developing their own questions. It doesn't apply to every situation, but it does apply to a lot.

4) Question Cards. If you are working with a learner who is really struggling to come up with their own questions, try creating a set of question cards. These are a set of cards containing model questions, question stems, subjects for questions and anything else you can think of which might be relevant. The learner can then use these cards when trying to come up with their own questions.

5) Questions to Choose From. If you have a learner who finds the whole process of question formation almost too difficult to manage, you can still support them. When you want them to come up with their own question to direct the learning, square the circle by offering them a choice of three questions you've developed. While this means the learner isn't coming up with the questions themselves, it does still ensure they have a degree of independence and can feel in control of what is happening.

What questions would you like to be able to answer?

Consider this:

Teaching Assistant: We're starting a new topic today looking at plants. What questions would you like to be able to answer by the time we finish the topic?

Learner: I'd like to know why there are so many different plants. Where do they come from? I'd also like to know why flowers are so pretty. Is there a reason that flowers are pretty? And I want to know what we can do to look after plants. What's the best way to protect the environment so plants are protected?

This is a lovely technique to use at the start of a topic. It helps learners think about what they want to know, do, learn and understand during the course of the lessons ahead.

Following on from our example, we can imagine the teaching assistant making a note of the questions their learner comes up with. The teaching assistant and learner can then refer to these questions during the course of the topic. They can try to answer them and use them as a tool for checking how the learner's understanding is developing.

Using this technique means giving learners a chance to take control of their learning. It is also motivational because it helps learners attach their own meaning to a topic of study. In this example, it's likely the teacher has planned lessons which will cover the questions the learner has come up with. But by having the learner decide their questions independently, the teaching assistant has found a way to bind the learner into the learning, making it more personal to them.

Summary

In this chapter we've looked at five techniques you can use to differentiate your questioning. These are:

- Using the concrete to abstract continuum to underpin your questions

- Using the general to specific continuum to underpin your questions

- Using 'show me, tell me, convince me' to structure your questions

- Helping learners to develop their own questions

- Asking learners 'What questions would you like to be able to answer?' at the start of a topic

Chapter 8 – Increasing the Level of Challenge

In the introduction I made the point that differentiation is about helping all learners to access the work, regardless of their starting points. It's about helping all learners to make great progress and it's also about ensuring all learners have an appropriate level of challenge. The majority of the book has focused on strategies and techniques you can use to support learners who are struggling to access the learning, or who are having difficulties with the lesson content.

In this chapter we can spend a bit of time looking at five techniques you can use to increase the level of challenge. These techniques are appropriate when learners are finding the work too easy. This might be because they have mastered the lesson content or it might be because they are already familiar with it – perhaps the current lesson isn't as much of a challenge for them as it could be.

Make it More Complex

When learning is more complex, it tends to be more challenging. If you have a learner who is finding the work too easy, you can increase the level of challenge by increasing the level of complexity. Here are two ways to do it:

1) Introduce a caveat. A caveat is an extra requirement a learner has to fulfil as part of the task they are doing. For example, you might be working with a learner in a geography lesson. They have been asked to sort a series of migration factors into two piles – push and pull. They have done this quickly and correctly. So, you introduce a caveat to make the task more complex. You say: 'I'd now like you to sort them into two piles, but also make sure each of the piles is ranked from most to least important.' Now the learner has to revisit their piles and change the order of the factors so they are ranked from most to least important.

2) Pose an additional question. If a learner is whizzing through a task, try posing them an additional question intended to increase the level of challenge. These questions should be more difficult than the rest of the task. The aim is to slow the learner down and cause them to think more deeply about what they are doing. For example, in a science lesson you might be working with a learner who is speedily moving through a series of questions about forces. At this point you step in and pose an additional question to increase the level of challenge: 'What if you had to explain each of your answers in more detail, using more keywords? How might they be different?'

Both of these techniques rely on you slightly changing the task the learner is trying to complete. The extra element you introduce makes things a little more complex for the learner. This increases the level of challenge and pushes the learner to think differently about what they are trying to achieve.

Synthesis Questions

Bloom's Taxonomy is a hierarchy of cognitive processes outlining the thinking learners are asked to do in school. It has six levels: Knowledge, Comprehension, Application, Analysis, Synthesis and Evaluation. Each level is more complex than the last. Comprehension is harder than knowledge, for example. And analysis is harder than application. The top two levels of the taxonomy are synthesis and evaluation. These represent the most difficult thinking learners will have to do about a topic. Synthesis means to create new things or put existing things together. Evaluation is about assessing or ranking things.

You can increase the level of challenge for your learners by posing them questions based on synthesis or evaluation. We'll look at the latter in the next entry. Here, we can focus on synthesis.

Synthesising information means taking what you know and using it to create something new. That might be something completely new or something which is just a little different from what you know already. Here is a list of synthesis keywords:

Combine, Compose, Construct, Create, Devise, Design, Formulate, Hypothesise, Integrate, Merge, Organise, Plan, Propose, Synthesise, Unite.

You can use these keywords to come up with synthesis-based questions. You can use the keywords directly, or you can use them as inspiration for questions which ask learners to be creative. Here are six examples of such questions:

- Can you create a poster showing how photosynthesis works?

- How might you combine the ideas of trust and cooperation into a logo?

- Can you propose a way to build a new wildlife garden?

- What if you had to come up with a different way to cross the river? What would it be and why?

- What sort of plan can you suggest for dealing with the problem?

- If you had to design a solution to climate change, what would it involve?

Each of these questions challenges learners to think creatively – and that is the essence of synthesis-based questions.

Evaluation Questions

Evaluation is the top level of Bloom's Taxonomy. This is a complex cognitive process. We have to weigh up the strengths and weaknesses of something, its pros and cons. Having done this, we then need to come to a decision about the thing in question – and provide a rationale for that decision. For example, in a history lesson a learner might be challenged by the teacher to evaluate the relative usefulness of a series of sources. To do this, the learner will have to look at all of the sources, compare them to one another and then decide which are more useful and which are less useful – and why.

You can use keywords to come up with evaluation questions, before using these questions to increase the level of challenge your learners are faced with. Here is a list of evaluation keywords:

Appraise, Argue, Assess, Critique, Defend, Evaluate, Examine, Grade, Inspect, Judge, Justify, Rank, Rate, Review, Value.

And here is a set of six exemplar evaluation questions:

- What might be the best argument for limiting greenhouse gas emissions and why?

- How would you defend the idea that change is always a good thing?

- Can you rank the items from most to least valuable?

- Can you justify that?

- If you had to decide whether security is more important than freedom, how would you do it?

- How would you assess your contribution to the lesson?

You can use evaluation questions to increase the level of challenge for your learners. Ranking is often an easy route to go down, especially when there are a number of things learners can evaluate. For example, they could rank a set of sources, a set of images, a set of ideas, a set of arguments, or a set of books, using different criteria in each case.

Ask the Learner to be the Teacher

Teaching can be quite a challenging process. One of the most challenging aspects is taking a large amount of information and finding a way in which to present that information to an audience. Teaching is in large part about communication. The communication of ideas and information. For communication to be effective it needs to be clear, precise and thought through.

You can increase the level of challenge for your learners by inviting them to become the teacher. This means asking them to teach you about something they've learned. The challenge comes from the fact that the learner now needs to look afresh at what they've learned and think about how they can re-present it to you, in a way that will help you to understand it.

You can increase the level of challenge by playing dumb – by pretending that you don't know anything about the topic. By doing this, you put all the onus on the learner. They have to go into greater detail and communicate more clearly if they are to successfully teach you about what they have learned.

For example, a teaching assistant might be working one-to-one with a learner in a numeracy lesson. The learner is racing through the work, getting everything right. The teaching assistant realises that the level of challenge for the learner is probably a bit low at the moment. As the learner finishes their work, the teaching assistant steps in and says: 'Pedro, you clearly know your stuff on this topic. I can see you've answered all the questions pretty quickly and got them all right. Can you explain the topic to me? Can you play the role of teacher?'

You can also use this technique when you are working with a small group of learners. For example, you might ask one of the learners to teach the topic to the rest of the group. Or, you might invite all the learners in the group to take turns teaching the topic (or part of the topic) to each other. In both cases, the learners involved benefit from the challenge presented by having to take on the role of teacher.

Just a Minute

There is a popular BBC Radio Four light entertainment programme called Just a Minute. It is a gameshow in which four competitors (usually comedians) take it in turns to try and talk about a subject for one minute, without deviation, repetition or hesitation. If someone is talking and they deviate from the topic, repeat themselves or hesitate, other competitors can buzz in, identify the error and then take the topic on themselves.

You can adapt Just a Minute to stretch and challenge your learners. If a learner completes all their work in quick time and doesn't appear to be particularly challenged by what they've been asked to do, try playing the game with them. Challenge them to talk about the topic of study for one minute, without deviation, repetition or hesitation.

Explain what each of these terms means and give the learner a chance to think about what they will say, then start the timer.

At this point, there are two options open to you. First, you might play the game in such a way that whenever the learner deviates, hesitates or repeats a word or phrase you stop them and challenge them to try again. Second, you might keep count of the mistakes the learner makes during sixty seconds, then tell them their score at the end. You can then invite them to have another go. This time they must try to beat their score from the first round.

The game is lots of fun. It focuses learners' minds as they have to think carefully about what they are saying and how they are saying it. The challenge is to convey as much information as possible, without falling foul of the rules around deviation, hesitation and repetition.

Summary

In this chapter our focus has been on how to increase the level of challenge. We've looked at five strategies you can use to do this while you're working with learners. They are:

- Making the learning more complex

- Posing synthesis-based questions

- Posing evaluation-based questions

- Asking the learner to take on the role of teacher

- Playing the 'Just a Minute' game with your learners

Chapter 9 – Retention Strategies

Some learners have difficulty accessing learning because they struggle to retain information. This has a couple of implications. First, the learners meet new learning with less solid foundations than some of their peers. Second, the learners can find their working memory overloaded as they are having to devote processing power to a wider range of things than their peers.

For example, we might have a learner who is finding religious studies difficult. As part of this, they have struggled to retain the keywords and important information the teacher has been teaching them over the last couple of lessons. If this learner is then asked to complete an activity or assessment drawing on what they've learned so far in the topic, they are going to find things difficult.

First, they will be meeting the task with shakier foundations than other learners in the class. Second, they will not have the luxury of using their long-term memory for some sections of the work – because they've struggled to retain information there. This compounds their difficulties. They find themselves trying to think about everything at once and, as a result, their working memory becomes overloaded.

Let us look, then, at five techniques we can use to help learners retain information. These techniques help learners to access the learning by setting them up with stronger foundations on which to call and by giving them a better opportunity of storing information in their long-term memories.

Practice Testing

Practice testing has been shown to be a highly effective technique for aiding recall and retention of information (see the study conducted by Dunlosky et al in 2013). Practice testing is where learners practice recalling information in an environment or manner which is similar to a formal test, but with the removal of the high-stakes element. This is where we test learners on what they know, helping them to practice their recollection of information as they go. Because the stakes are low the stress levels are low. Hence the technique is conducive to learners feeling engaged and motivated.

Here are two examples of practice testing techniques:

- **Flashcards.** This is where you and your learners create a set of cards containing questions or cues on one side and answers on the other. The cards can then be used for practice testing. For example, you might be working one-to-one with a learner in Year 5 literacy lessons. The learner struggles with spelling and needs to improve their recall of how to spell commonly used words. So, you create a set of flashcards you can use to help them practice. On one side of each flashcard is a sentence missing the word the learner needs to spell. On the other side is the correctly spelled word. Of course, the learner can also use these cards to test themselves.

- **Frequent quizzing.** In this technique, you make quizzing a regular feature of your interactions with your learners. The aim is to give them lots of opportunities to practice recalling information – and to learn from their mistakes if and when they make any. For example, a teaching assistant might be working with a group of learners outside the main lesson, helping them with their writing. They might introduce a practice testing element by running a pop quiz at the start of every other session in which learners have to recall keywords or phrases they will later be writing about.

Spaced Practice

Spaced practice also scored highly in Dunlosky et al's study. This is where we plan a schedule of practice over time, giving learners a series of opportunities to practice recalling information, with gaps in between their attempts. For example, a teaching assistant might be working one-to-one with a learner during their GCSE science lessons. They decide to plan a schedule of spaced practice to help their learner develop their recall. It looks like this:

- Every first lesson: 7 question pop quiz on chemistry keywords

- Every second lesson: 6 question pop quiz on physics keywords

- Every third lesson: 8 question pop quiz on biology keywords

Notice how we see some similarities to practice testing. The key difference is that spaced practice is about practicing over an extended period, with gaps in between. So, in this example, the teaching assistant is going to test their learner's recall of chemistry, physics and biology keywords every three lessons. The spacing out of the practice creates variation and means the learner and the teaching assistant can get into a pattern – a rhythm, if you will – of practice.

You can plan spaced practice into your work when you know you are going to be working with a learner, or a group of learners, over an extended period of time. You might even want to liaise with the teacher so you can plan this together.

Another benefit of spaced practice is that you can teach the method to your learners. If, for example, you have a learner who wants to improve their retention of information and is willing to work on this at home, you can plan a spaced practice schedule with them, then ask for updates on their progress at regular intervals.

Semantic Interrogation

Our third and final technique from Dunlosky et al's study. Semantic interrogation also scored highly. This is where learners ask the question 'why?' They interrogate their learning, searching for meaning. Once they can attach meaning to what they are learning, it becomes easier to remember. This is because the learner is remembering both the information and the meaning of that information. It is also because the learner has been active in thinking about what they have learned. They have interrogated it and found a way to give it meaning.

Imagine, then, that we have a teaching assistant who is working with a small group of learners in a literacy lesson. The learners are analysing a poem. They need to show that they can pull the poem apart and explain the meaning of different elements. The teaching assistant challenges the learners to research the author of the poem. Why did they write the poem? Why were they interested in these themes? Why did they choose to write about this topic in particular? Why did they go for this style of poetry? Why did they choose the different poetical devices they did?

Why, why, why, why, why. The teaching assistant is helping the learners to semantically interrogate the poem. They are priming them to attach meaning to their analysis.

Encouraging learners to ask 'why?' means encouraging them to look for the meaning behind things. Once they find this meaning they can use it to gain a better understanding – and a securer retention of the lesson content.

An additional point to note is that if you identify ideas or information your learners are struggling to retain, try giving them reasons which explain why the ideas or information matter, why they exist or why they are relevant. This sees you doing the semantic interrogation on behalf of your learners and then sharing it with them.

Stories

We looked at the power of stories earlier, in Chapter Four. There, we thought about how we can use stories to explain ideas and information, helping learners to access the learning in the process. Here, we can think about how stories aid retention. How they help learners to retain what they've learned.

Some psychologists have argued that story-telling is an integral feature of what it means to be human and that humans have a particular capacity for telling and remembering stories. Whether this is completely true or not does not matter. What matters is that we understand the power of stories to influence learners when we are working with them.

Start telling a story to a group of learners and the chances are that they will automatically stop what they are doing and start listening. Stop that story before the end and you may well be met by a number of disgruntled faces.

You can use stories to help learners remember important information and ideas. Either wrap this learning up in a story or find a story that sits behind or connects to the information. For more on this, see the entry on stories in Chapter Four.

Another option is to train learners in how to tell stories about their learning. For example, you might invite a learner to turn what they know about photosynthesis into a story. This doesn't mean they need to make up lots of fictional things about the topic. Rather, it means they take what they know and put it into the structure of a story, giving it a beginning, a middle and an end. They can then focus on remembering the story, confident that in doing so they will remember the component parts – the key pieces of learning they have accumulated regarding photosynthesis.

Songs

Our final retention technique isn't for everybody. So only go with it if you feel happy that it's for you. It involves using songs. And it isn't guaranteed to work, but it does have a pretty decent pedigree.

We remember songs well. Consider how many songs you know. How many songs you could sing along to or hum along to if they came on the radio. Consider also the role of songs in helping very young learners to learn things like the alphabet and their times tables.

You can make use of the way in which we remember songs to help your learners retain information. Here are three ways you might go about it:

- Look for songs on YouTube aimed at learners. The Sesame Street YouTube Channel has a large number of such songs aimed at younger learners.

- Invite your learners to come up with a song or rap they can use to remember some of the things they've been learning about. For some learners this will be a great thrill. For others, not so much.

- Take a popular song you and your learners are familiar with and change the lyrics so they are about the most recent lesson topic. Share the song with your learners and invite them to sing it themselves, then to learn it off-by-heart or to have a go at making their own version.

As I said, singing as an aid to retention isn't for everybody. Arguably, it works better with younger learners. Perhaps because of the content of the songs, perhaps because of the lack of inhibitions these learners have when it comes to singing in front of their peers. It can be a useful technique, and it is one worth thinking about. See what you think – and see how your learners feel about it.

Summary

In this chapter we've explored a range of techniques you can use to help learners memorise and retain information. The five techniques are:

- Practice testing, including flashcards and quizzing

- Spaced practice, where we implement a schedule of practice

- Semantic interrogation, where we help learners attach meaning to their learning

- Using stories to aid recall

- Using songs to aid recall

Chapter 10 – Conclusion: Recapping and Next Steps

And so, we bring our exploration of differentiation to a close. We began the book by defining differentiation. Now is a good time to remind ourselves of some of the things we said:

'Differentiation is all the ways in which teachers or teaching assistants help learners to access the learning, regardless of their starting points. It is about personalising learning...all the strategies and techniques teachers and teaching assistants use to ensure the learners they are working with can make good progress, no matter what the lesson topic.

Differentiation for teaching assistants means finding strategies and techniques through which they can help learners to access the learning and make good progress during the lesson. It is about the interactions teaching assistants have with learners. These interactions form the basis of the teaching assistant's work. It is through interactions that they help learners, support them and work with them.'

Throughout this book we've looked at what this means in practice. We've done this by examining a wide range of strategies and techniques you can use to personalise learning for your learners. We've ranged over a large area of classroom practice – because differentiation covers all the things we can do to help learners access the work, not just some of the things. While we haven't been able to cover every last aspect of differentiation, we have covered a lot. And there are many practical ideas ready and waiting for you try out.

We've looked at a whole host of strategies and techniques you can use to help learners access the learning and feel a sense of personalisation. In short, we've looked at how to differentiate effectively. Let's recap this here, by bringing all of the strategies and techniques together in one place for ease of reference:

Chapter Two: Essential Techniques for Personalising Learning

- Connect learning to learners' prior experience so they can make sense of it and use their existing knowledge and understanding to access the learning

- Simplify the work learners have to do so it is easier for them to get to grips with

- Break the learning down so learners can tackle one thing at a time

- Help learners attach meaning to learning so they understand why they are being asked to do things and have greater motivation to engage with the work

- Create opportunities for learners to experience success so as to foster a positive engagement with the learning

Chapter Three: Verbalising Thinking

- Verbalise your thinking, giving learners access to your expertise

- Discuss tasks with learners so they can edit, order and refine their thinking

- Discuss questions with learners so they can practice articulating and revising their ideas

- Discuss strategies with learners so they can verbalise their ideas about how to tackle challenges

- Use discussion to precede writing. This means learners can edit, order and refine their thinking before transferring it into the written word

Chapter Four: Approaches to Explanation

- Use images to supplement verbal explanation and as an alternative source of explanation

- Re-explain ideas and information to learners to help them understand what the teacher has explained to the class as a whole

- Use stories as an explanatory device and to help learners remember ideas and information

- Give examples so learners have something concrete to hang onto. Examples also help learners build up a more detailed understanding of a topic

- Use analogies – they have many strengths when it comes to explanation. At the same time, be aware of their weaknesses as well

Chapter Five: Scaffolding Strategies

- Help learners to use memory extensions such as scrap paper and mini-whiteboards

- Help learners to use a variety of classroom tools to self-scaffold

- Start learners off with their work. This does a little bit of the work for them, giving them a way into the learning

- Suggest options from which learners can then choose

- Use prompting and clueing to help learners access the learning

Chapter Six: Modelling Techniques

- Model thinking so learners gain access to your expertise. They can borrow from this, copy it and imitate it, helping them to refine and improve their own thinking

- Model strategy selection so learners understand how to use appropriate strategies

- Share model sentences with learners. They can then use these as a starting point for developing their own writing

- Use exemplar work as a reference point from which learners can borrow

- Model positive self-talk so learners can change how they think and feel about themselves and their learning

Chapter Seven: Differentiating Your Questions

- Use the concrete to abstract continuum to underpin your questions. Concrete questions are simpler, abstract questions are more difficult. Move along the continuum in response to how learners respond.

- Use the general to specific continuum to underpin your questions. General questions are easier to answer than specific ones. Move along the continuum in response to how learners respond.

- Use 'show me, tell me, convince me' to structure your questions. 'Show me' is the easiest part of the strategy, 'Convince me' is the hardest part.

- Help learners to develop their own questions. Use techniques such as sharing model questions, sharing question stems, 5Ws and 1H, question cards and giving learners a selection of questions to choose from.

- Ask learners: 'What questions would you like to be able to answer?'

Chapter Eight: Increasing the Level of Challenge

- Make the learning more complex, for example, by introducing caveats and by posing additional questions

- Pose synthesis-based questions which invite learners to think creatively about the lesson topic

- Pose evaluation-based questions which invite learners to think critically about the lesson topic

- Ask learners to take on the role of teacher. Increase the challenge by playing 'dumb' and putting all the onus on the learner to explain and teach the learning to you

- Play 'Just a Minute' with your learners. Challenge them to talk about the lesson topic for one minute without deviation, repetition or hesitation

Chapter Nine: Retention Strategies

- Use practice testing, including flashcards and quizzing

- Use spaced practice, where you implement a schedule of practice for your learners

- Encourage semantic interrogation, where you help learners to attach meaning to their learning

- Use stories to aid recall – learners can remember the story and, by extension, its constituent parts

- Use songs to aid recall – learners can remember the tune or the melody and associate words with this

And with that, we draw things to a close. Let me conclude by wishing you good luck in your efforts to personalise learning for your learners. Good differentiation makes a real difference to how learners access learning. It can transform their experience of the classroom, empower them and help them to make much better progress than would otherwise be the case. By using the strategies and techniques in this book, you'll be supporting your learners in their efforts, and giving them every chance of being successful. I'm sure you'll do a great job.

Select Bibliography

Anderson, Lorin W.; Krathwohl, David R., (eds), *A taxonomy for learning, teaching, and assessing: A revision of Bloom's taxonomy of educational objectives*. Harlow: Pearson Education, 2014

Black, Paul; Wiliam, Dylan, et al, *Assessment for Learning: Putting it into Practice.* Maidenhead: Open University Press, 2003

Bloom, B. S.; Engelhart, M. D.; Furst, E. J.; Hill, W. H.; Krathwohl, D. R., *Taxonomy of educational objectives: The classification of educational goals. Handbook I: Cognitive domain*. New York: David McKay Company, 1956

Bruner, J., *Acts of Meaning.* Cambridge, Massachusetts: Harvard University Press, 1990

Bruner, J., *Child's Talk: Learning to use Language.* New York: WW Norton & Co. 1983

Bruner, J., *The Culture of Education.* Cambridge, Massachusetts: Harvard University Press, 1996

Cummins, J., *Language, Power and Pedagogy.* Clevedon: Multilingual Matters, 2000.

Dewey, J., *Experience and Education (Reprint edition).* New York: Touchstone, 1997 [1938]

Donaldson, M., *Children's Minds.* London: Fontana, 1978

Lemov, Doug, *Teach Like a Champion.* Hoboken: Jossey Bass, 2010.

Mercer, N., *The Guided Construction of Knowledge: talk amongst teachers and learners.* Clevedon: Multilingual Matters, 1995

Mercer, N., *Words and Minds: how we use language to think together.* London: Routledge, 2000

Petty, Geoff, *Teaching Today: A Practical Guide.* Cheltenham: Nelson Thornes, 2004

Printed in Great Britain
by Amazon